Midcentury

Midcentury

BEN HOWARD

Ben Howard

SALMON POETRY

Published in 1997 by
Salmon Publishing Ltd,
Cliffs of Moher, Co. Clare

A catalogue record for this book is available from the British Library.

Salmon Publishing gratefully acknowledges the
financial assistance of the Arts Council.

ISBN 1 897648 74 X Softcover

Cover design by Estresso
Set by Siobhán Hutson
Printed by Redwood Books, Kennet Way, Trowbridge, Wiltshire

To the memory of

Marion Curtis Howard

(1905-1971)

and

Johanne Elizabeth Howard

(1902-1984)

Other Books by Ben Howard

POETRY

Father of Waters: Poems 1965 - 1975
(Abattoir Editions. The University of Nebraska at Omaha. 1979)

Northern Interior: Poems 1975 - 1982
(The Cummington Press, 1986)

Lenten Anniversaries: Poems 1982 - 1989
(The Cummington Press, 1990)

PROSE

The Pressed Melodeon: Essays on Modern Irish Writing
(Story Line Press, 1996)

Acknowledgements

'The Word from Dublin, 1944' first appeared in the *Sewanee Review* (vol. CII, no. 2, Spring 1994). 'Stone on Stone' received the *Milton Dorfman Prize* and appeared in the newsletter of the Rome Art and Community Centre (Rome, New York). 'Spitting Forgiven' first appeared in the *Seneca Review* (vol. XXIV, no. 2, 1995) and 'The Centre of Attention' in *Chelsea* (59). The poems have also appeared as limited editions, printed by Jerry Reddan and published by the Tangram Press of Berkeley, California.

I am grateful to those friends who have read the poems in typescript and offered valuable suggestions. Special thanks to Mary Beckett, Philip Booth, Carol Burdick, Hayden Carruth, Robin Caster, Marilyn Chin, Henri Cole, George Core, Daniel Davidson, Michael Davitt, Stephen Dunn, Clare Dunne, Richard Foerster, Eamon Grennan, Christine Grontkowski, David Hamilton, Michael Heffernan, Dillon Johnston, Alan Littell, David Meissner, John Montague, Wendy Parsons, Edward Power, Jerry Reddan, Michael Stephens, and Deborah Tall. Thanks also to Jessie Lendennie for editorial advice, to Heather Yanda for proofreading, and to Pat Sweeney for secretarial assistance.

For its support of this project I am indebted to the National Endowment for the Arts. I also wish to thank the Centrum Foundation, The Corporation of Yaddo, and the Tyrone Guthrie Centre (Annaghmakerrig) for providing the inviolate solitude in which some of these poems were written.

Contents

I

The Word from Dublin, 1944

I greet you from a neutral country in a neutral hour.

Robert Greacan

The neutral island in the heart of man.

Louis MacNeice

I

I can't begin to say what brought me here,
Unless it be the Irish predilections
For whiskey and horses, both of which entail
A certain risk and a less-than-certain gain.
To be a middle-aged American
In Dublin in the middle of a war,
Of which we're hearing more or less than nothing,
And that in fragments, bits of veracity –
A mutilated bulletin, a headline –
Is to see one's lot reflected in the stories
That come to us distorted, if at all:
Stories of heroism, sacrifice,
Or, more often, utter devastation.
Of Irish horses I know next to nothing.
Of Irish whiskey I can claim the knowledge
Given to those who can't pretend to know
The subtle processes of distillation
By which a grain becomes a thing of beauty
And a *force majeure* in decimated lives
But know too well the amber Irish jewel
That shoots its radiance though heart and soul
And soothes the brains it hastens to dismantle.
Water of life indeed – its irrigation
Useful to a spirit somewhat parched
By human frailties and human needs
Or, more specifically, the final exit
Of her whom I was pleased to call my wife
Until I called it quits and left those scenes
Of mutual defeat and exploitation

3

And she, in concert, left for Colorado,
Taking her parrots and our only child.
Or, more recently, my troubled lover,
Savagely beautiful but off her rocker,
Who also bolted, taking neither child
Nor furniture but much of my belief
In sanctity and high-romantic logic.
Reasons enough to sojourn in a country
Notorious for its hospitality,
Itself no stranger to intestine wars
But neutral where the lunacies of Hitler
And the blusterings of Churchill are concerned –
And to find some consolation in a landscape
Which in the evenings sometimes calls to mind
The saintly scholar's tranquil countenance
Of, if you like, the monks at Clonmacnoise
Transcribing psalms and jotting marginalia
In perfect peace, before the Danes' arrival.

II

The heart has many corners, but this city
Is, I think, a diagram of corners,
Not least the pungent snugs of the Palace Bar,
Those corners where the heart can talk itself
Out of its misery or celebrate
Its minor triumphs over a ball of malt.
That last is Irish for a shot of whiskey,
A phrase I fancy only a little less
Than the thing itself, mainly because it captures

The truth about the permanence of things.
For what that trick of speech is calling solid
Is really liquid, not precisely formless
But certainly susceptible to change,
By which I mean consumption, disappearance.
On that one point, if nowhere else, the Irish
Remind me of those smiling Buddhist monks
Who make impermanence their daily meditation,
Along with suffering, the formless ego,
And the spectacle of loved ones' flesh decaying.
For death, as the poet said, is never far
From the Irish mind, or ever very far
From the darker corners of the Palace Bar,
Where sometimes in the evenings I allow
My thought to circulate around my father,
That stout Midwestern Methodist, whose leading
Scruple was a stern sobriety
In talk as well as drink. *Weigh your words,*
He told me – sound advice, if seldom taken,
And seldom needed, now that certain words
Carry more weight than anyone can manage.
'What's eating *them*?' I asked my sober sister,
Noticing, off to the side, two upright farmers
Standing at attention like those Gothic
Oldsters in the painting. 'Don't you know,'
My sister said, 'They have *moralysis*.'
That was a dream, some thirty years ago.
I *didn't* know. How *could* I, having grown
Almost to manhood with that same affliction,
Which causes Iowans to see the world
As more coherent than it really is

And gamely to construct a moral dream
Where black is black, and a promise is a promise?
In the nether corners of the Palace Bar,
Where black is seldom black, or a fact a fact,
My father's dream can seem a kind of madness.
And just to keep my bearings in this country,
Whose ancient language has no words for Yes
Or No, but only subtle shades of meaning,
I sometimes scratch the facts on sodden napkins:
I'm forty-eight. My son is nine. Tonight
Is June twenty-second, nineteen forty-four.

III

What is the colour of neutrality?
Here, on a bright morning, Dublin Bay
Could be the mind of a contemplative,
So still it is and so remote from news
Of warring states and hostile polities.
Pewter or silver, depending on the light,
It gives the lie to factions, quarrels, feuds –
Those hovels where we live and have our being.
My own mind, in truth, is anything
But still. If I were looking for its emblem
I could do worse than find it in those trees
That greet me every morning: crazy shapes,
At once preposterous and rational,
Purposeful and random. Look at them
For any length of time, and watch them write
A script in cockeyed Sanskrit characters,

A cryptic homily on Art and Nature,
Their green angles going north-northeast
And south-southwest – suggestive, to be sure,
But just as surely indecipherable.
Monkey-puzzle trees: as good a name
As any for a mind that knew its place
Some twenty years ago, but now suspects
Its place to be those waters where the mines
Drift in their testy, lethal isolation,
Until some joker from the Port Control,
A scruffy, wizened sot with iron nerves
And a view of life inclining to the comic,
Skewers them gently on his ten-foot pole,
Unhooks their circuitry, uncorks their acids,
Extracts their charges and their moving parts,
And dumps the whole affair in Dublin Bay.

IV

How I became a lexicographer
Is anybody's guess, and how I came
To ply my trade in languid Ireland
Is a riddle someone else can solve.
Perhaps it was the challenge of a culture
Where furniture and families seldom move
But language is as fluent as the light
On Dingle Bay, and speech is parabolic,
Informing by degrees or not at all.
And can you tell me why a Methodist
By birth if not exactly by deportment

Should gravitate so often to St. Patrick's
And there, if not to pray, at least to sit
In the attitudes of prayer, achieving nothing?
Simple in purpose, grandiose in form,
That nave could be the soul's intelligence,
Reciting its enigmas in a language
Of strut and boss and marble definitions.
So, too, the Dean of savage indignation,
Interred beneath those tables where the tourists
Riffle the cheap brochures and ochre postcards,
Could be the listener who hears our whispers,
The echo when a folding chair is folded,
The scrape of soles on stone. His noblest thought,
Dispersed in his parishioners' defeats,
Their chronic blunderings and peccadilloes,
Could be that aisle in a silent hour.
And I confess: I like the thought of Swift
Lashing the Irish for their foolishness,
Not with a sermon from his bully pulpit
(Which even now could scare our feathers off)
But with a charitable irony:
The gift of his estate to build a nuthouse
Because, said he, the Irish needed one.
The heart, it seems, survives on contradictions,
Paradoxes, polar opposites,
Which, as any smiling monk could tell you,
Are, or ought to be, the provenance
Of laughter. Nonetheless, I wasn't laughing
The afternoon my smiling erstwhile lover,
Back for a little fatherly advice,
Showed me the photos of her plaintive suitor.

Naked, melancholy, bunion-eyed,
He looked less ready for a night of love
Than for a therapeutic overhaul.
'He isn't well,' I said, too sick at heart
And too confused to make a smart remark.
I haven't seen her since, except in dreams
And even then, strangely transmogrified.
In one, she flew directly through my window,
Flapping her wings and begging my forgiveness.
As it turned out, it wasn't she at all
But a yellow parrot, odious and spectral,
One of the minions of Her Ladyship,
Squawking *I told you so, I told you so,*
And flying off, its hunger satisfied.

V

Let me define a word for you: *erasure.*
Its root, *radere,* means to *scrape*; its prefix,
E, means *out.* Hence, a *scraping out.*
Its closest synonyms – *efface, expunge,*
Delete, cancel, and *obliterate* –
Approximate its meaning but miss out
Its modern connotations: blackboards, sponges,
A gentle rubbing, leaving a trace or smear
Indicative of error, misdirection,
A change of mind, a wise reversal. Once
On Kildare Street, on a Thursday afternoon,
As I made my way to the National Museum,
Clicking the black gate that separates

Irish antiquities from Irish streets,
I shuddered – not out of pity or regret
Or anything so noble as respect,
But out of a sudden sympathy for myself,
Remembering, as I did, those multiple
Erasures. Youth and faith. My daffy lover . . .
A senile mother, speaking words aloud . . .
Luckily for me, I snapped myself
Out of that bootless fit of self-absorption
And took my tour of the National Museum,
Viewing erasure on a larger scale,
By which I mean the ruthless, systematic
And mere erasure of the Gaelic order.
Necklaces and bracelets, pendants, rings,
The Ardagh Chalice and the Tara Brooch –
Those relics only underscored the sad
Finality, the pathos of it all.
I told you so, a parrot might have said
To Hugh O'Neill at the Battle of Kinsale,
That armature on which a culture swivelled,
Gathered speed, and spun into extinction.
And again *I told you so* to those ripe souls,
The self-made martyrs of the Easter Rising.
Their letters, uniforms, and diaries,
Their tiny pistols raised against an empire –
What lesson there, except it be the lesson
That wild courage, careless of its losses,
Can teach the rest of us – we cautious ones,
Who know too much, or have too much to lose?
I moralise, I know. I have no right.
But just the other night at the Palace Bar,

I heard the tale of the O'Rahilly,
Mortally wounded in the insurrection,
Who dipped his finger in his own life's blood
And daubed his R.I.P. on a Dublin doorstep.
'Now *there's* presence of mind,' my inner cynic
Started to say – until my inner critic
Rebuked him harshly for his glib remark.
And then my heart, pumping itself for combat,
Offered the less-than-startling observation
That truth and courage drink from a common well.
And last, my judgment, having the final say,
Reminded all of us that youthful men,
Dying without regret for their beliefs,
Are not more foolish than the spectacle
Of unbelieving sods in drafty tweeds
Sipping their whiskeys and their pints of Guinness.

VI

Call it the light of things awakening
In late July, the light on water trembling
Beneath the overpass, the furtive light
That is no younger than the crumbling stone
But nonetheless deceives you into seeing,
In water splashing rock, in water threading
A path through channels smaller than your hand,
A ghost of youth, a phantom of renewal.
Whatever it is, it's come belatedly
To me, as to this neutral, youthful nation,
Which after two millennia may yet

Bestir itself from De Valera's dream
Of purity and perfect isolation
And find, despite its national inertia,
Its place among the nations of the world.
If what we've heard from Normandy is true
The world may soon have cause for celebration,
If also cause for vengeance, cause for mourning.
As for me, I spend my waking hours
Compiling the unlikeliest of books,
An Irish lexicon, and writing long
Inconsequential stories for my son,
Who, if anyone, can still be neutral
And still believe in leprechauns and fairies.
And sometimes when the sun is coming up
I look out on the waters of the bay
And dream of drifting mines, and count my blessings,
And measure my success in Irish miles.

II

Stone on Stone

Dingle Peninsula, 1945

We are all now dispossessed.
Paul Muldoon

I

I wonder whether poverty or water
Is more to be feared – the first so dangerous
To health and happiness, the second likely
To drown our sorrows with the rest of us
And leave our children permanently poor.
After a hampered year in Dublin City
I've settled here – a foreigner as always
But certainly no stranger to the sound
Of water splashing in a whiskey glass
And water supping freely on the rocks
Fronting the wild sea at Dunbeg Fort,
Which are to all appearances removed
From any danger of impermanence
But are, when all is said, as vulnerable
As you or I to gradual extinction.
It wasn't innocence that prompted me
To rent this house in Ballyferriter
And so remove myself from urban noises
And urban pleasures – innocence, that is,
Of human tricks and natural disasters.
Call it a hunger. Or call it something old
And spacious in the basement of the psyche,
A recreation room where fallen gods
And nascent hankerings disport themselves
In motley colours, blathering all the while
Of purity and imminent renewal.
To that perennial recuperation
This place could be the answering refrain,
Itself a stomping-ground, an injured party

With fifty centuries of habitation
Under its belt and more than one defeat
To test its fortitude and call its own.
A little short of cash but long on relics,
It lives on memory, as some of us
Subsist on lust, or thrive on desolation.

II

How did it happen that the two of us
Fell out, our bodies seeking private quarters,
Our spirits separate retreats? Not
The best of friends, we nonetheless remained
For all intents and purposes a marriage,
Founded not in Heaven nor in Hell
Nor in the cruelties of youthful passion,
But in the mutualities and causes,
Common or otherwise, that make dependents
Out of the most unfriendly nation-states
And from the brass of sheer necessity
Fashion a leash, or forge a brazen chain.
I was her father, she my surrogate mother.
I was her innocent, her new arrival,
Stuffing her vacant nest but less than pleased
To draw my breath beneath that pile of feathers.
Thus our analyst explained the case,
Fighting, I thought, bewilderment and boredom.
And in the end his costly clarities,
Such as they were, availed us very little
And were as nothing next to broken glass,

The sucker punches, mostly below the belt,
The savage insults, never to be forgotten.
Following custom more than inclination,
I packed my bags – and thus became the latest
Volunteer in that uncomely legion,
The regiment of fathers dispossessed
Of hearth and armchair, dignity and stature.
Watching the waves at Ballydavid pier
I think of nothing – nothing except the night
I came as stranger to my own front porch,
Wearing the mantle of the absent father.
Better to think of nothing than to dwell
Too long on that abrupt humiliation
Or see again my child's frightened eyes
Watching behind his mother's flaring skirt –
Or hear again the crashing of that door
With all the vengeance of her grief behind it
And all the solemn majesty of the law.

III

Where are the relics of the dispossessed?
Here at the tip of this peninsula,
Remote from Churchill's boasts and Hitler's bombs,
I've come upon more relics than the heart
Can plumb or fathom – remnants of other wars,
For which the mutilated ogham stones,
The souterrains of promontory forts,
The fractured castles and the signal towers
Are but the fragmentary signatures,

Sealing a contract long since breached and scattered.
Here where the light is changing every second,
It startled me to come upon a relic
Unchanged by centuries of dislocation
And held intact by gravity alone.
But there it was – the Gallarus Oratory,
An empty chapel built of corbelled stone,
As featureless and naked as a mound
Of rubble, save that its sides and roofline rose
Into a silhouette of praying hands
Or, if you like, the contours of a hull,
As though those lonesome eremites had chosen
To chant their matins in an upturned boat
And put their comforts permanently on hold.
Stranger though I was, I liked the strangeness
Of corbelled stone – no mortar there, nor brick,
Nor even moss to add a little colour.
What were they saying, those uncommon stones,
Those planes and edges? Maybe that the heart,
Made pure if rather chilly by devotion,
Will outlast even massacring armies?
To such exalted sentiments I once
Subscribed, and might again, should those conditions
Which gave them privacy and sustenance
And sheltered them from God-knows-what disaster
Be reinvented under sun and rain
Or replicated well enough to trick
The undiscerning eye. Stepping inside
That dark surround at seven in the morning,
Its eastern window framing the Atlantic
Its western door a lookout on the mountains,

I thought of rampant Danes and ruthless Normans –
And saw that curious inverted vessel
Sailing through twelve unnerving centuries,
Its freight no heavier than deathless faith,
Its cargo not a cache of spoiled fish
But strict observance, stern and undefiled.
Cold and a little dank, that dwelling-place
Seemed less a chapel than a vestibule,
Where those of us with nowhere else to go
Might linger, singing no fervent litany
And staving off the siren-songs of dogma,
But leaving nonetheless with passions stirred
And the weight of memory a little lighter.

IV

And now the strangeness of the days advances,
Not in a rush but with a steadiness
That rattles me – as once the river's water,
Dropping beneath the weight of my canoe,
Awakened fears I'd rather not remember.
That happened of a summer afternoon
Some thirty years ago – a nice surprise
For one whose innocence was still inherent
And who for all his brooding had no clue
To the certainties of loss and deprivation.
Watching that early version of myself
In memory, I scarcely recognise
The silly kid who blundered into Lock
And Dam 13 on the Mississippi River

And felt the water like an elevator
Lower itself and him with no more warning
Than might be granted to an alcoholic
Just on the brink of scotching wife and child
Or some incorrigible adulterer
Undoing love with the dialling of a number.
Here on an island's bleak extremity,
My son and I a hemisphere apart,
I feel again that blank, enormous wall
Banging against the hull of my canoe
And the slime-hung rope by which I held my own,
The water draining steadily beneath me,
As down a shaft or foul-smelling hole.
It was, I think, my earliest intimation
Of sudden loss and self-inflicted wounding,
Of which all later acts of dispossession,
Sudden or gradual, imposed or chosen,
Were but a clear and rueful confirmation.

V

There is a bitter, eremitic joy,
Grounded not in touch or conversation
Or in the colloquies of loving friends
But in the sure repose of sand and stone
And the poverty of silent contemplation.
Hardly the one to munch on watercress
And chant myself to sleep between cold stones,
I tip my hat to those intransigents,
Those wily Gaels and self-negating monks,

Who could have given in but chose instead
To build their huts in this forsaken place,
Their little beehive huts, devoid of bees
But swarming with their vows and abnegations.
Theirs was not a militant resistance,
And the preservation of their Oratory –
So vulnerable to storms and demolitions –
May be a happenstance, a stroke of luck,
A baffling oversight of Cromwell's armies.
Nevertheless, I find in their condition
An emblem of my own, and in their chapel
A mentor for my unbelieving mind.
Certain of very little, I'm convinced
That memory itself is mortarless,
Its elements no larger than a hand,
Its hut a curvature of jointless stones.
Lost in the nestings of my monkish bed,
I relish, now and then, those ruptured stones,
Which are, when all is done, my true possessions,
Crude as they are by ordinary standards,
Dark as they are by ordinary light.

III

The Mother Tongue

Co. Kerry, 1946

I am accustomed to their lack of breath . . .
W. B. Yeats

I

    With not a word of Irish to my name
And no more purpose than befits a maker
Of etymologies and definitions,
I've brought my books and papers to this place,
Where field and furrow speak in Irish phrases
And English is at best an afterthought,
At worst a numb and merciless invader,
Who saw his own reflection in the landscape
And left no word or name inviolate.
Across the water, more than one invader
Has left the field, discovered suicide,
Or heard at Nuremburg the final word
On genocide and brute imperial power.
But here in County Kerry, English words
And English names perpetuate a story
Retold at every cottager's expense
And written in the bent, bilingual signs
Which take it as their mission to mislead
The traveller, or otherwise impede
The next imperialist, the next invader.
And underneath the skewed phonetic spellings,
The conqueror's confused approximations,
There runs a speech as fluent as the feeling
Of loss itself – a feeling not unknown
To a forty-nine-year-old American
Whose recent history has more in common
With a long bout of Spanish influenza
Than with the confidence of British voices
Intoning plaudits over their pile of rubble.

27

Another harmless drudge, I hear my fortunes
Echoed not in Standard English timbres
But in the rise and fall of Irish voices,
The earthy consonants and liquid vowels,
The supple and mysterious ellipses
Of a tongue that has for centuries lamented
Its banishment to zones of stony soil,
And fashioned out of memory and pity
A parable of ruth and Gaelic glory.

II

What is a mother tongue if not a vessel,
Impervious to rain but vulnerable
To ruin? Here in the *Gaeltacht*, smashed and scattered
Over the rocky fields of western counties,
The mother tongue resembles nothing more
Than bits and pieces of an ancient vase,
Whose sturdy clay reliably contained
The truths of saga, balladry, and song,
The cold ferocity of poets' curses,
The seacoast dirges and the *sean-nós* cries
And crazy Sweeney warbling in his tree.
And though each shard retain the history
And half-remembered grandeur of the whole,
The whole has vanished into empty air,
Condensing here and there in mound or dolmen,
In passage-graves and rings of standing stones.
But while I'm thinking of the mother tongue
I can't help adding that apostrophe

Which bears the freight and onus of possession
And makes the mother tongue a mother's tongue –
That tablespoon and weapon of destruction,
So fit for nurturing or rendering,
For feeding open minds and trusting eyes
Or ripping infant psyches, limb from limb.
All of this by way of introducing
That savage moment from my childhood
When Mother, having heard of my affection,
My childish crush on someone else's daughter,
And having heard from me the prototype
Of all my later lovesick declarations,
Retailed my story to her next-door neighbours
And spilled my innocent, untried desires
Over the coffee cups and playing cards,
The chocolate wafers and the word Canasta.
In a small corner of that living room,
Recoiling from the blow of that explosion,
I listened to the voice of an announcer
And heard in low, authoritative tones
That I could be sure if it was Westinghouse.
For a long time, I curled up on a cushion
Repeating that insinuating phrase.
But decades on, I'm sure of very little,
Except that in the passing of a moment
And the passing of my words across the table,
I learned the bitter truth of violation,
The first invasion of the private heart,
And learned against a child's deepest wish
That I could love but never trust my mother.
Walking the sandy beach at Brandon Bay,

Its warmth a solace to my calloused feet,
I call upon those waters to remove
The last contusions of that primal hurt
And speak across an arc of forty years
The words of peace and the phrases of forgiveness.

III

Ochone! Ochone! the Galway women cry
In the old play, their voices calling up
A sunless coastline and a rocking curragh,
A melody embellished by the knowledge
Of loss on loss, and inconsolable sorrow.
Better, I tell myself, to take a walk
Or take a drink, than conjure up the image
Of misspent hours drowning in their bath
And one's own talents stumbling to their graves.
Yet even now I find myself reminded
Of the afternoon I traipsed, a little shaky
From too much solace in my whiskey glass
And too much jesting with mortality,
Into that cemetery, half-alert
For signs and omens. Cloon na Morav it
Was not: no meadow there, nor broken slabs,
Nor headstones listing in their sunken mounds.
No highflown crosses either: only granite,
Cut and toned with modern instruments
And set in rows, neat as a baker's dozen.
They might have been the titles on a bookshelf –
Name after name, distinguished not by stature

Nor even by their dates of publication
But by the evidence of wear and tear,
The weathered letterings and faded hues
By which the generations sort themselves
And the youngest stand indubitably apart.
Inspector General or connoisseur,
Reviewing troops or savouring the taste
Of strangers' names and strangers' epitaphs,
I came upon the oddest of them all:
Máire McCarthy, 1895
To 1925. And just beneath
Her dates, inscribed in Roman capitals,
As if in keeping with its permanence,
Was her address: *20 Emmett Street.*
Maybe it was the whiskey in my heart
Or the wings of angels beating in my brain,
Or the amber afterglow across the headstones –
Whatever it was, it prompted me to wonder
If what I'd witnessed was the residue
Of Máire McCarthy's precious time on earth
Or, more likely, Máire's last address
To which all correspondence might be sent,
Now and forever, return receipt requested.
What had I stumbled on, if not a village
Whose habitants were never to be seen
But always to be found at their addresses?
And who was I, if not the awkward caller,
Welcome or unwelcome, taking names
To which I had no right and no connection,
Except it be the fact of their condition,
And the quiet poignancy of their addresses,
Speaking themselves in rows of coloured stone?

IV

Mother was not the sort to magnify
My failings, gross as they were, and not the one
To punish me overtly or directly
For sins against the gods of Common Sense
And the deities of Reasonable Behaviour.
Her *modus* was a tacit disapproval,
A dexterous and lateral manoeuvre
By which the ball of wax was deftly passed
Across to its creator, namely me.
Putting my drab supper on the table,
Her back bent in a posture of submission,
She dished out more than meat and mashed potatoes.
'It's *your* funeral,' she liked to say,
Enforcing by that apt exaggeration
The scruples of a Methodist, who fancies
Himself the cause of each abomination
That comes his way, and keens himself to sleep
On misplaced griefs and sorrows not his own.
Every now and then, I think of her
Mopping the floor and muttering her contempt
For fops and wastrels, hypocrites and fools.
But what was I thinking of that afternoon,
Driving through the precincts of Listowel,
The weather not the best for making choices,
The rain a subtle register of doubt?
Cursing the rain, I parked my borrowed car
In the town square, facing the iron gate
And the iron palings, black as any frock,
That kept their sober church apart from traffic.

And then I left, returning hours later
To find my car mysteriously surrounded
By other cars, my exit blocked entirely.
Uncanny is the word for what prevailed
That afternoon – a close, uncanny silence,
Where no one spoke or ambled through the square
And the soft rain sustained an atmosphere
Of penitential grief and absolution.
Was it the weather or the silent men
Who slouched outside the pub, their caps and coats
Dampening in the rain? Or was it I,
Who summoned up the mourner in myself
And left the dry interior of my car
To stand among some others in the square,
Folding my arms, as if to watch a race,
Or hear a speech, or judge a boxing match?
After a time, undoing all pretense
Of knowing where I stood or what I stood for,
I asked a *garda* what was going on.
'A funeral,' he said. 'A mother of nine.'
And then we chatted for a little while,
Exchanging pleasantries and anecdotes,
And fending off the presence of the mother,
Whose coffin had already come to light
And now was winding through the open gate,
Borne on the shoulders of her son, her brother,
And others whom the *garda* could have listed –
They and their families, for generations.
Seldom have I felt more fraudulent
Or more in violation of the codes,
The histories and shibboleths that bind

A parish to an image of itself,
A culture to its own reclusive centre.
Unwitting, well-intentioned, inadvertent –
Was I not the latest incarnation
In a long line of ignorant invaders,
Meeting the Irish on their own terrain?
It was *not* my funeral and never would be,
Though what I saw of foreign lamentation
And foreign tears collapsed all definitions –
Their grief my grief, their lineaments my own.

V

O holy longing. Not the turn of phrase
To please a querulous apostate. Not
A sentiment to generate belief
From one who had the calling to dismantle
Those articles of faith on which his rocker
Lifted and dipped – those wicker certainties
On which he'd sat, thinking himself complete.
'Too serious by half,' the lady said,
Herself unburdened by those borrowed griefs
And rented grievances which sometimes drive
My conscience into alien terrain.
But once again, the lady was mistaken.
Solemn as I can be, and sometimes am,
I've seldom shown the seriousness that questions
Its own proclivity to questioning
And entertains, if only for a moment,
Its gravest hints and holiest of longings.
Such is my regret this Sunday morning,

The weather rueful even by Irish standards,
The damp parishioners in hats and scarves,
Their faces redolent with absolutes,
Leaving their place of sanctity and worship.
We hew and delve, but when it comes to matters
Too intimate for rational dispute,
I fear the virulence of definitions,
The intellect's unsparing violations.
Beyond this island, nursing their ghoulish wounds,
The nation-states adjust their boundaries,
Composing polities and mapping bridges
Over disparities of race and creed
And making out of multiple invasions
A not-so-just and not-so-stable order.
Hearing the tongues of bells proclaiming peace
Over an increment of Irish rain,
I ask myself how often I've invaded
The sanctities I scarcely understand
And by the analyst's inquiring hand
Done harm without and violence within.
What is a grievous loss if not the faiths
Of childhood invaded by the knives
And needles of the sceptical adult,
Who has, for all his self-condoned intentions,
Divided soul from body, heart from mind,
And left himself bereft of his address
Or any promise of a lasting home?
Ochone! Ochone! for those unruly phantoms,
Those fantasies of innocence and order,
Which even now accompany the sight
Of narrow streets and fractured paving-stones
And foreign recusants returning home.

IV

Spitting Forgiven

Dublin, 1947

After such knowledge, what forgiveness?
T. S. Eliot

I have you, and I'm more than grateful to you. But sure I'd expect no less from you. You're all nature.
Brendan Behan – *The Quare Fellow*

I

Having a staunch affection for this city,
Where gas was rationed not so long ago
And brewing a cup of tea at certain hours
Was tantamount to brewing bootleg whiskey,
I've spent a winter in a furnished flat
Just north of Sandymount, my whiskey warmed
By water from a steaming, legal kettle.
So many laws were broken by the tanks
And bayonets of troops across the water,
It seems a piece of moral sophistry
That here in Ireland a pensioner
Could find his pension nicked, his honour dented,
For heating a little water on the sly –
Or, as the Dubs would have it, *on the glimmer*.
Grey bread, grey paper, hoarded food and petrol,
The ration-books that told us *There's a war on*,
Have vanished with the coming of the English,
The young Parisians strolling Nassau Street,
The menus in the window of the Gresham,
Which give the passing tourists the impression
Of enviable prosperity and calm.
What lingers from that old austerity
And catches my professional attention
Is not so much the relics as the phrases
Which have a life and vector of their own.
To be a Yankee lexicographer
Among the Irish is to have one's ears
Bombarded with the likes of *hoor* and *stocious*,
Which have their share of meaning for the talkers

Who occupy the benches on the green
But have no home in any lexicon
And leave a Yankee's thirst for definition
Unsatisfied, his palate teased and thwarted.
With not enough to show for fifty years
And plenty to remember and regret,
That's not the only hunger I've brought with me
To Ireland – this home for desperadoes,
Who've lived for several centuries on the glimmer
And seem, at times, to savour desperation.
Just yesterday a Dubliner informed me
That a *glimmer* was a residue of gas
Left in the pipes, after the valves were closed –
Enough to brew a pot but not enough
To cook a meal or heat a clammy home.
And at the door, at any time, could come
The *glimmer man* – the dour Gas Inspector,
Checking the jets for signs of indiscretion.
With all such practices and deprivations
I feel a certain mutuality,
Having myself subsisted on the whiffs
Of old theologies, and having lived
For decades in a state of disapproval,
Of moral dread and imminent remonstrance,
As though the spirit's fuel were illicit
And the Glimmer Man were just around the corner.

II

You'll see me in my coffin, Mother said,
Too many times to reckon or recall.
But always the occasion was the same:
Some piece of disobedience on my part
Or act of cruelty – if cruelty
Is quite the word for boyish misdemeanors,
For filial neglect and indiscretion,
Some foible of ingratitude, for which
The punishment was not a reprimand
Spoken in haste and hastily forgotten
But that reminder of our rendezvous
Somewhere in the near or distant future.
Uttered with disgust or with a touch
Of prophecy and certain retribution,
It seldom failed to conjure up the image
Of Mother on her back, bedecked with flowers
And resting at an awesome elevation.
Nor could it fail to sketch across my conscience
The spectre of myself as thankless child,
Whose just deserts would certainly include
Removal of the small and selfless mother
Whom he had failed, repeatedly, to cherish.
Would that she had slapped me once or twice
Or blistered me with flaming imprecations
Than that her words, spoken with such restraint
And such disdain, should percolate through decades.
Which in the slow chronology of the soul
Could be a century. And need I say
That on the winter evening when she kept

Her promise, wearing a simple floral blouse,
Her features irretrievably reduced
By widowhood, decrepitude, and illness,
Her rouged cheeks suggestive of a circus,
I couldn't begin to say whose vindication
Had come to us at last, or whose comeuppance
Dwelt in the rank odours of the flowers,
The hushed condolences of relatives,
The muted anecdotes in which her kindness
And flawless love were gratefully remembered.

III

What is the name for that capaciousness
Which duly notes a drunkard's thickened speech
And sees a lecher wheeling out of orbit
And hears a liar's mangling of the facts
But still extends its welcome to the culprit
And offers a warm seat beside the fire?
Here in Ireland they call it *nature*,
By which they mean no pastoral seclusion
But quite the opposite – a gross immersion
In human messiness and imperfection,
The oversights that botch the perfect wedding,
The phones that seldom work, the clocks that can't
Agree or tell the truth, the mail that has
A will of its own, arriving when it pleases.
And, beyond all that, the brutal failings,
The dark malignities. Walking the beach
At Bray, my heels unsteady in the sand,

My beard regaled by another Irish drizzle,
I thought of the little signs on Dublin trams
Declaring their improbable proscription.
Spitting forbidden, they warn the traveller,
As though the smoker's most forbidding habit
Were more containable then Irish rain –
Or less promiscuous than human malice,
Which drops its parcels, when and where it chooses.
Would that all those mailings might be gathered
Into a carton marked *Return to Sender*.
And would that all the spittings of those madmen
Who called themselves *il Duce* and *der Führer*
Had been forbidden by some higher power
Before their virulence became endemic,
Their spittle lethal. Tale by horrid tale,
The stories of the massacres and death trains,
The images of wholesale executions,
The testaments of skeletal survivors,
Have made their way through folds of insulation
And have, for some of us, assumed the stature
Of household gods and secular mementoes,
Reminding us – even at this remove –
Of moral voids and unforgivable evil.
Yet even as I say that, I'm recalling
An evening spent in Ennis, County Clare,
The lights low in a dusky music hall,
The *sean-nós* singers weaving their plaintive stories
Of sons and fathers lost, of families
Destroyed by waves and fatal human choices.
Strange as it may seem, what caught my notice
And stirred some dormant knowledge in my blood

Was not so much the singers' nasal voices,
Their liquid trills and miniature cadenzas
But what erupted from their audience –
Or, if I may steal a forlorn word
Out of my childhood, their *congregation*.
Indigenous and mostly in their fifties,
Their faces grooved, their eyes exuberant,
They knew the words and melodies by heart.
And when their voices joined the choruses
An octave lower, reminding me of thunder,
It seemed the voice of some volcanic passion
Contained in stone – the voice of suffering,
Replete with grief and cognizant of anguish.
It was – or so I thought – the voice of *nature*,
Forgiving fate and fatal human error –
Or the voice of humankind forgiving God
For each new loss, each bloated casualty.

IV

My father held his own behind a curtain
Of reticence and patient understanding –
Not the sort of curtain one could part
Without an effort, a yanking at the cords,
A noticeable friction in the pulleys,
A stopping-short. And I was not the one
To crawl beneath those folds of crumpled velvet
Where no one, even I, had been invited.
In that respect, I was my father's child,
Preserving someone else's privacy

As though it were an article made sacred
By years of awe and silent veneration.
Odd that my father's voice should come to mind
Just as I was crossing Nassau Street,
Thinking not of Methodists or silence,
Much less a Methodist's unnerving calm,
But of the etymology of *stern*,
Its roots in *star* and Viking fortitude.
Odd that in the din of cars and lorries
A son should hear a voice entirely vanished
Except in memory and meditation –
A stern but melancholy baritone,
Judicious to a fault, but not without
The registers of tenderness and sorrow.
Odder still that as I made my way
Around the narrow curve of Grafton Street,
What should present itself but something risen
Out of the ashcan of my childhood,
As if to admonish me or call me home.
But there I was, alone, before my father's
Office door, its window painted black.
And there, against that interstellar void,
Its ten injunctions framed in red and gold,
Its code set down in gilded Roman letters,
Was nothing milder than the Decalogue –
My father's notion of a welcome mat,
Greeting me with its promise of remorse
For stolen dimes and nickels, mindless pranks,
The daily mischiefs of a nine-year-old
Who took the Ten Commandments seriously
But often failed to mention his misdeeds

And sometimes framed them, even to himself,
As accidents or trivial moral blunders,
Better to be forgotten than reproved.
It wasn't long before the blare of traffic
And the jostlings of the shoppers on the sidewalk
Undid my reverie and ushered me
Back to the slanted light of Grafton Street.
But what that moment's vision left me with
Comes back to me in dreams, as though that blackness
Were not a curtain but the man himself
And the ten Reminders posted on his window
Were the features of the ghost who fathered me
And to this day reminds me of my failings,
Even as he guides me down a sidewalk
Littered with coins and scraps of foreign paper.

V

Seldom short on moral absolutes,
Oliver Cromwell had the clarity
And the artillery to simplify
The world into a diagram of Evil
At odds with Good – of Protestant and Devil,
The armoured Gall and the ill-defended Gael.
Generous in his way, he offered captives
The options of extinction or departure.
To Hell or Connaught? Thus his righteous soldiers
Set forth the choice in no uncertain terms,
So certain were their consciences, so plain
Their God's imperatives. But driving north

From Drogheda one day, my dirty windshield
Deflecting blasts of slanting Irish rain,
I saw my own imperatives as less
Than plain, my rights and wrongs as less than certain.
Watching the pubs and shops define themselves
Through undulant meridians of rain
I thought of Cromwell's armies marching south
And saw, if I may say it, all those slaughtered
Victims of his absolute convictions,
His self-convinced and self-protective cleansing
As just so many pebbles in a delta,
So many shells and splinters strewn in mud –
And saw his cold morality as water
Carving its jagged scar across the landscape,
Its narrow channel emptying at last
Into a spacious, all-consuming basin,
A place of openness and indirection,
Of undertows and coiled, conflicting currents.
Hospitable or otherwise, those waters
Have offered rest, if not exactly solace,
And seem, at times, my natural habitat.
In any case, it's there I found myself
One winter morning, my brain but half-awake,
My body aching and my vision circling
Around a twisted, decomposing relic,
Its punctured hull and barnacled remains
Disclosing nothing of its origin
Or history, its ill-considered venture.
Shining a light inside a crumbling porthole,
I saw the signs of human habitation –
Corroded knives and forks, some broken plates,

A mound of chairs, a heap of pots and pans,
The residues of griddles, vats, and kettles,
And on the floor, assorted skulls and bones.
That last sufficed to waken me entirely
And send me lurching toward my morning coffee.
But as I watched the steam above my cup,
Its little knots unravelling to nothing,
I thought that what I'd glimpsed inside that vessel
Was less an emblem for my own condition
Than for the wreckage of a century.
Fortunate to have lived beyond the reach
Of Lord Protectors, Potentates, and Führers,
I nonetheless have quarrels of my own
With the entourage of priests and absolutists,
The robed authorities and moralists
Who occupy my reveries and dreams
And would – if I would let them – have their say
In all my diatribes and admonitions,
My muted gibes and silent condemnations.
There is, in short, a Cromwell in myself
Who's not embarrassed by his own pronouncements,
Which have as their foundation nothing more
Than scrapped conjectures, jettisoned beliefs,
Discredited theologies and bits
Of moral speculation, spat from God-
Knows-which defunct religion. In small, a pile
Of junk, a moral landfill. *Here I stand*,
My conscience sighs, *and I can do no other*,
Even as I sink beneath my weight
Into a reeking mass of rusted metal.
Could you not be more forgiving of yourself?

The lady asked. To which I said, 'I could.
But let me first forgive my century,
Which chipped away all semblance of belief
And gave us Dresden, Belsen, Hiroshima –
To name a few – and isn't over yet.'

VI

Something possessed me of a Friday morning
To ride the bus from Dublin to Armagh,
Leaving, as it were, the seat of commerce
For the brain of temporal authority
And the bald head of patriarchal power.
Watching the shifting light above the drumlins
And the stony fields of County Monaghan,
I felt a darkening within myself
And in that megalithic Northern landscape,
As though a voice were deepening by the mile.
And after that, Armagh, its apple orchards
Sifting the chaff of amber Northern light.
Eden it was not, but looking out
On the stands of apple trees, their well-pruned branches
Heavy with ripened fruit, I sensed the presence
Of innocence and imminent fulfilment.
Beyond the orchards came the town itself,
Its newly painted shops, its sudden hills,
And on my left and right, its twin cathedrals,
Catholic and Protestant, respectively.
Around the latter one, some scaffolding
Signified attention and renewal –

Or, if you like, a vote for preservation.
Watching a scruffy mason pointing stonework,
A workman hauling buckets up a ladder,
I thought of other schemes and restorations
And what's been going on across the water –
The bombed-out cities picking up the pieces,
The nation-states arising out of rubble.
Returning home, I called to mind a dream
I've had not once, but often: myself out walking
In shorts or wraps, depending on the weather,
The field before me overgrown with weeds,
And my own steps uncertain. And then a room,
A chamber, rather. The smell of plaster dust.
The taps of mallets in a vacant choir.
And overhead, a net of ribs and bosses
From which the graven faces frown and smile.
Misericordias, or some such motto,
Allures me to a solitary corner,
And there, amidst a momentary whiteness,
An ambience of faith without an altar,
I recognise that fabric as my own.
Call it a half-built temple or cathedral,
Or something yet to be identified
And yet to shed its light upon its maker.
Spitting forgiven, I would have them mount
Over the door of the confessional –
Or better yet, the meditation hall,
Where once a day I'd take my threads of malice,
My coiled dreads and animosities,
My mother's angers and my father's laws.
And there, beneath a window left ajar,

I'd watch those knots unravel in the languors
Of late afternoon, as though the force of *nature*
Had caused their old solidities to vanish,
Their rancours to dissolve in liquid light.

V

The Centre of Attention

Co. Monaghan, 1948

I

Across the water it was called the War,
But here in Ireland, where parachutes
Redeemed from wreckages were resurrected
As silken blouses, silken skirts and scarves,
The Irish called it the Emergency,
At once reducing its significance
And lending to the gists of common things –
To tillage, turf, paper, bread, and petrol –
A patina of worth and urgency.
It's all in how you see it, I suppose,
But after half a decade in this country
I've come to wonder if my way of seeing
Is not as fixed as that of Irish farmers,
Their backs to the Atlantic and their eyes
Converging on the coulter and the furrow.
What motive did I have in coming here
Except to make a book of roots and meanings,
A small, Hiberno-English lexicon,
And in the process find a little solace,
A welcome respite from those urgencies
Which might be called, for lack of better words,
My private War, my soul's Emergency?
How fitting that a lexicographer
Of modest birth and dubious distinction
Should bring his woes and homely pigeon-holes
To an island that eludes all definitions
And seek relief from chronic self-delusion
In an ambience where passions and obsessions
Are not so much exceptions as the rule.

Five years on, I've made but little progress
On either project, having nothing more
To show for all my efforts than a heart
As prone as always to befuddlement
And stacks of scribbled notes, as yet unordered
And less than lucid, even to their author.
What better mirror for a bungled life
Than sheafs of synonyms and antonyms
Recorded with meticulous precision
But written in a hand unduly fine –
A pile of useful, useless information
Which grows a little deeper by the day
And which, if I should die before I wake,
Will be at best a present for my son,
A tribute to his father's misdirection,
A monument to scholarly attention
At odds with chaos and the rush of time.

II

Where did it begin, that cast of mind
Which sets its painted idol at the centre
Of each new circumstance? Which wrenches each
New thought into a vector of devotion
And spurs the votary to squander hours
And dollars in the service of a mistress
Who will, if true to form, abandon him,
Withdrawing by that act the very rug
On which he paid preposterous obeisance?
I'm sure that if I knew, I've since forgotten.

But could there be an inkling in this landscape,
These fields that wear the colours of abstention?
Here in County Monaghan, these drumlins
Took on, just yesterday, a chastened light,
A cold though oddly human character
Which chilled my spine and nudged me to remember
A moment from my ambling adolescence
When the balusters and clapboards on my street
Went dark, and trees that had companioned me
Through half my childhood suddenly looked strange.
As it happened, what had charged their leaves
With an eerie green and made their shadows black
Was nothing more uncanny or unwonted
Than an annular eclipse – my first and best,
Of which all others have been replicas,
Or parodies, or answering refrains.
But was there not an emblem in that moment,
Or should I say a lesson for the stumbler
I was and am – that inward-gawking pilgrim
Who in his first and second adolescence
Coloured the world with what he thought was passion
But was, in truth, a blotting of the sun,
In aspect marvellous, in substance normal,
Its beauties gorgeous but ephemeral?
Under the influence of that convergence
Of sun and moon, nothing was what it seemed,
And what it seemed was grossly simplified,
Its features doctored preternaturally.
How else explain the late October morning
When she and I were riding on a train
To Boston, both exhausted, both in need

Of something stronger than our morning coffee –
Something to clear our heads and clean our lenses
And show us to each other, warts and all.
I have the grace to blush when I remember
That at the time I'd dubbed her My Beloved,
Misnaming both desire and its object
And puffing in her face a kind of vapour
Through which she drew her breath as best she could.
And I was forty then – a little late
For making goddesses of common mortals
Or lowering a spiritual tiara
On anyone's unkempt, bewildered head.
Yet lower it I did, and more's the pity,
For while I turned my efforts to installing
Halo after halo on her brow
I must have missed a thousand other things-
The rocking railway car, the passing landscape,
The conversation in the seat behind us,
The negro porter gliding down the aisle.
I do remember, now, a dowager
Who thought that we'd eloped, and told us so,
And another, drooping low, exuding talcum,
Who inquired if the lady might be sick.
Other than those two, I can't remember
Anything at all of our environs,
So keen was I on tending to the needs
And savouring the grace of my beloved,
Who by this time had fallen fast asleep
Though not exquisitely, a glob of jam
Adhering firmly to her open mouth.
Cocked back against her headrest, looking less

The goddess than the victim of assault,
She stirred and snored – a noise, that had I heard it
For what it was, might well have been a klaxon
Warning of disasters yet to come.
And had I then the prescience to decipher
The message in her hard, downturning mouth,
The portent in the cracks beneath her makeup,
The cold self-hatreds hiding in her eyes,
I might have spared the two of us the anguish
Of savage separation – she departing
A few months later, wanting nothing more
Of my relentless, spotless adulation,
Which was at first her sustenance and joy,
A radiance exceeding her deserts,
But was at last a noisome silhouette,
A crazed intruder blocking out the light.

III

The mad attract their like, the poet said,
Referring to a killer and his cohort,
Two officers with pistols on their belts
And murder on their minds, who carried out
What others only dream or think about:
The shooting of a prisoner at dawn.
Not that he'd committed any crime.
Rather that he'd found himself the target
And the occasion of a killer's fit,
A useful outlet for a passing anger.
Nor was his case all that unusual,

His fortune so abnormal on this island,
Which has for fifty centuries impounded
The addled wits of numberless fanatics,
The homicidal fantasies and deeds
Of lunatics, indigenous and foreign.
And if indeed the mad attract their like
I've wondered more than once why I've been drawn
To a nesting-place of fantasists and dowsers,
Of cunning indolents and outright rogues,
Among them Grace O'Malley, piratess,
Who flung her enemies from parapets
And held, if what the ballads say is true,
Dominion over men of savage mood.
Never the one to shrink from mortal combat,
She grew too old to wield her two-edged sword
But satisfied her lusts by other means,
Appearing on the poop deck in her nightgown,
Her streaming hair and shimmering apparel
Sufficing to intimidate the sailors
Who took her for a ghoulish apparition.
There is, I'm sure, a pirate in my psyche
Who's spent a night or two with Irish phantoms
And quickens to the tale of Grace O'Malley,
Who's had a tryst in every century
And every county of this chthonic country,
Where freedom is a visionary dream,
A nubile aisling flirting with her maker.
Nor can the likes of Truman, Eisenhower,
Roosevelt and Franco hold a candle
To the overarching spectre of Cuchulain
Straddling the giant ring at Emain Macha

Or the warm ghost of Medbh in Connemara,
The cattle-stealing queen whose appetites
For sex and conquest pulsate in the mists
Above the bogs, outlasting Mussolini.
Whether they be the workings of the gods
Or the tricks of hypnotists, those ghostly forms
Could tell an ancient, cautionary story
And knock a little sense into a Yankee
Who's spent a lifetime watering ideals
And spared no pains in parenting delusions.
I could be grateful for the deep repose
Of History and Factuality –
Those stone pavilions where I hold dominion
Over my own unwashed, unruly moods.
Instead I find myself in Ireland,
Where poets still intuit holy light
Around the whins, and statues of the Virgin
Bestir themselves in radiant undulations.

IV

A lot of snash and blathers, snapped the curate,
By which I mean the lout behind the bar
At the Black Bush – my temporary parish,
Where some of us had gathered to replenish
Our stores of knowledge and percipience,
Opining freely on the foolishness
Of Chamberlain, the excellence of Rommel,
And drifting over several pints of Guinness
To the Gaelic pastorale of de Valera –

That western paradise where handsome hurlers
And virgin maidens gambol in the sun.
The innocence of that Edenic vision
Elicited the curate's interjection
But woke in me a kindlier response,
Bringing to mind the image of my son
In bathing trunks, and prompting me to wonder
Yet again at my propensity
To train my purest, fiercest concentration,
My mind's engine and my heart's desire
On the one thing that can or will not stay.
How transient the hour when I stood,
Expectant, at the bottom of the slide
To watch him mount the ladder, step by step,
And at my urging, hurtle down the chute,
Fear and delight commingling in his eyes.
What was it but a second innocence
To watch his first adventures on the rug,
His shaky steps and partial comprehensions –
Or to hold him steady while he ventured out
Ten feet, then twenty, on his yellow bike
And having gained his balance, rode alone?
How transient the hour when I told him
The story of The Dragon Who Ate Stars,
While overhead the glowing constellations
Pasted to his ceiling faded out
And he himself devolved into his dream.
Of course it would have opened over time,
That gap between a father and his son.
But for the two of us those hours ended
Abruptly with Her Ladyship's departure

And what is called a legal separation,
Its violence undoing what was woven
With tact and patience, hour after hour.
I must have had a notion it was coming.
It must, in fact, have occupied my mind
Unconsciously the afternoon we wrestled
On the warm sand and played our favourite game,
A test of skill invented by myself
And aptly titled Knocking Daddy Over.
The rules were simple. I would sit crosslegged,
As if beneath the Bodhi tree, and he,
Taking a run of twenty feet or more,
Would fling his body's flying, flailing weight
On Daddy, who would gamely topple over,
Lifting him by his torso as he passed,
A tiny glider wafting into sand.
That afternoon I changed the rules a little,
Stopping his progress and the flow of time.
What was it but my effort to arrest
The present and to fortify the moment –
My choosing on an impulse to impede
His passage and immortalise his flight,
Holding him aloft against the sky
And framing, if I could, the moving face
That was, in small, a mirror of my own?
How lasting and how delible his laughter.
How transient that moment in the sun.

V

The days are often grey in Ireland,
Wet and grey and shameless in their changes,
An atmosphere conducive to reflection
And even more to Etymology,
Which might be called the poor man's excavation,
A kind of dentistry whose main concern
Is not the mouth's internal mastications
But what's come out of it for centuries –
Those little statesmen with their histories
Of want and need, intelligence and folly.
I think it was the first of my obsessions
And of them all, the one least capable
Of wreaking harm. To happen on a word
Unknown to you, or better yet, a word
Grown destitute and wantonly familiar,
Is to find a well, replete if not quite holy,
Wherein the senses may refresh themselves
And the cloistered self redouble its reserves
Of human history and human meaning.
I could have been no older than fifteen,
An innocent in every way but one,
When I uncovered, more by accident
Than conscious will, the lineage of a word
Which in my ignorance I'd thought remote
But as it happened, fit me to a tee.
The word was *silly*, as in *silly sheep*,
Which nowadays means trivial or foolish
But once meant weak or poor or pitiable
Or something similar to innocent.

That small discovery, the first of many,
Came back unsummoned not so long ago,
As I was driving on the road to Clones,
A lonely drive at seven in the morning,
The sullen hills encroaching on my car
Or seeming to, the sky a leaden blur.
Perhaps it was the power of suggestion
Or just the newness of that August morning,
But as I passed the little tillage fields,
The clouds of rhododendrons on the verge,
I found myself reentering the stark
And dusky confines of my father's study,
Reopening his books and leather journals,
And browsing in the pages of his O.E.D.,
Their textures dry and brittle to the touch.
And as I found again those definitions,
The page of meanings listed under silly,
I felt again the tremor of excitement,
That fervour in the presence of a word,
As though the word and I were made anew.
Call it the power of recovery,
By which a life that has exemplified
The finer nuances of silliness
Was briefly reconnected with itself,
Its wounds sutured and its fractures healed.
Call it what you will, that unrelenting
Revenant stayed with me through the morning
And trailed me through the narrow streets of Clones,
Whose chief distinction is a Celtic cross
Positioned at the centre of the town
And seeming by its prominence to draw

The pubs and shops to its circumference,
The sidestreets into attitudes of worship.
Ten centuries of manifest erosion
Had worn away the figures in its panels
But left the traces of their grimaces
And the outlines of their forms, suggesting struggle.
Had I been more at ease or better tutored,
I might have seen those markings as themselves
And read that massive emblem as a nexus
Of pagan faith and Christian sacrifice.
But in the filter of my changing mood,
Whose hues were turning darker by the hour,
That lofty monument, so long on meaning
But short on modesty, seemed nothing less
Than Memory itself, obstructing traffic
And casting shadows on the rest of us
And managing, as usual, to place
Its awful freight at the centre of attention.
A lot of snash and blathers, I would call it,
But for the fact of its continuance
And the sheer weight of its magnificence,
Its place among the graves and graven stones.

VI

Across the Water

Dublin, 1950

What is more fluid, more yielding than water?
Yet back it comes again, wearing down the rigid
strength that cannot yield to withstand it.
Lao Tzu

I

'Ah, she was a terror for the flowers.'
My neighbour smiles, recalling how his wife
Would watch their daily progress in her garden,
Blaming herself when dahlias failed to bloom.
Ever the guardian of buds and stems,
'She had no gift for leaving things alone.'
After a lonely year in Monaghan,
I've brought my aging ghosts to Dublin City,
Its streets at once familiar and foreign.
Nightly I take my walks through Sandymount,
Passing the terraced houses and the tight,
Well-tended gardens. And only yesterday
I found myself a tourist in the grey
And barren sameness of the new estates,
The spreading suburbs at the edge of town.
Whether or not the world is growing smaller,
It's evident that time is moving faster,
At least for me, and that my century
Has passed the midpoint of its long career,
Its innocence decreasing by the hour.
Reared with a reverence for conscious will
And its rewards, I pass my days in doubt
Whether to trust my fortunes to the cumbrous
Scaffoldings of methodologies
Or the white waves of faith and intuition.
'The water will hold you up,' our gentle teacher
Assured us at the outset of our lessons,
His features doubled in a tranquil pool.
That happened more than forty years ago,

But in the quiet lanes of Sandymount
His reassurance still reverberates.
Seldom the one to act on such advice
I've spent no little part of my reserves
Flailing against my visible support,
As though by taking arms against the weight
Of water I might keep myself intact
And by the impetus of will alone
Propel my burden to the other shore.

II

It could have sprung up almost anywhere,
That fantasy in which the static parts
And random movements of the outward world
Are brought beneath the fantasist's baton,
And all that happens, happens by command,
Its outcome no less certain than the mind
That fashioned it, the hand that waves the wand.
In me, it surfaced at the age of seven
Or thereabouts – a vague, peculiar dream
In which the doors and drawers in my room,
The knobs and switches, curtain-pulls and latches,
Were lashed together by a web of string,
A network no less dense than intricate,
And I, the sole creator of that net,
Was also its divine intelligence,
Its monitor and spider-puppeteer.
Propped against the wall, I pulled the cords
That flipped the switches, dimmed or doused the lights,

Opened and closed the closets, drew the blinds.
And though that fantasy could not have lasted
More than a day or two, its paradigm
Has made its way through four ensuing decades,
Inhabiting the kitchen where I cook
Four things at once, or governing the pen
With which I sign all things contractual,
Or lending to those powers of persuasion
With which I would restore the moral order,
An air of authority. How curious
That I should bring my frugal disposition
And calibrating mind to Ireland,
Where buses sometimes run on schedule,
And pubs are seldom known to close on time,
And time itself can trickle to a standstill,
Alarming no one. How sane it would have been
To set my tender roots in native soil
And stay within the reasonable extremes
And fertile decencies of Iowa,
Specifically that spot where Iowa
Bends the Mississippi. What better place
To propagate a rational illusion
And view the world as rectilinear,
Its codes no more ambiguous than those rows
Of corn, its highways regular and clear?
Yet even then there came from time to time
Reminders of the world's impertinence.
In one such instance, having wandered off
To a room in the Historical Museum,
A dusty home for military relics,
I came upon the ranks of youthful faces,

Each of them an Iowan killed in action.
Encased in glass and mounted on a spindle,
They might have been the blades of a propeller,
Revolving through my unaccustomed gaze
And whirling in my dreams for nights to come.
Closer to home, I heard the stories told
By fishermen and trappers – stories of corpses
Found in the sloughs or washed up on the sandbars,
Their faces changed beyond all recognition.
Closest of all, I heard one Sunday morning
The story of Michael Dunne, who lost his own
Battle with the Mississippi River –
Michael Marion Dunne, whom I had wrestled
Only the day before, and much too roughly,
Twisting his arm and yanking him to the ground.
'He never had a chance,' my mother said,
Sweeping the crumbs and wiping off the table.
Caught in the current and carried into the channel,
He might have struggled for a little while,
His fists clenched, his legs against his chest.
Whether it was that news or some disease,
I thrashed for seven nights, my fever rising,
My mind a screen of bright hallucinations.
In one I watched a rack of coloured balls
Explode in streams, struck by an oaken mallet.
And the night before my fever broke, I saw
A perfect sphere that might have been my soul
But was, so far as I could make it out,
A ball of string careening down the slope
Behind my school, unravelling as it rolled.

III

Weigh your words. That terse imperative,
So laden with its own significance,
Has stayed behind, its author long since vanished.
What weight it carried in my childhood
I couldn't say, commingled as it was
With other cautionary admonitions.
Don't jump off the porch. You'll break your arches.
Check your facts. Don't forget to signal.
Now, when I think of it, it brings to mind
The image of the two of us at cribbage,
His pointer not a fatherly pronouncement
But a tender nudge, a mild *obiter dictum*,
Attendant to his playing of a Queen,
His pegging forward. *Fifteen-two, fifteen-*
Four, fifteen-six, and a pair is eight,
And a pair is ten. And a Sunday afternoon,
Moving at the tempo of our pegs
Around the bend, our quiet competition.
How could I be other than who I am,
Having as my mentor that exemplar
Of weights and measures, counting out his hand?
Read 'em and weep – or merely tally them
And in the future try a little harder.
Yet in the backwash of a windy Friday,
Replete with showers from the Irish Sea,
I thought of him again – and not in the way
That others saw him – not the Principal
Whose presence, unannounced, could silence children
And bring a sudden pallor to the classroom –

But as the architect and engineer
Who built a stage-set for electric trains,
A plaster landscape, mountainous and stark,
And at the centre cut an oval hole
Where he would sit, surveying everything.
Perhaps it's just the layering of the years
Or the vagaries of memory compounding
Amalgams out of disparate events:
Whatever it may be, that fluent force
Has caused me more than once to see my father,
Content within the circles of his trains,
As the emblem of the father he became
In twenty years, his stricken body shrunken,
His hair abruptly white, his plans cut short.
Ringed by relatives and smiling friends,
Who'd made a tacit pact to reassure him
And not divulge the truth of his condition,
He lay confused and charitably betrayed,
His knowledge circumscribed by good intentions.
His only son, it fell to me to sever
The ligaments of that benign deception
And penetrate the folds of his illusion.
Never before or since have I more gravely
Weighed my words or watched their slow descent,
Their import settling darkly as they fell,
As though it were a shadow before a storm
Or water spreading freely over stone.

IV

How well the bandsmen keep us from ourselves,
The black anxieties and desolations
And the cold dampness of a Dublin morning
Dissolving in a Sunrise Serenade.
How well the voices on the wireless,
So thick with portent and authority,
Invent a solid, auditory world
Where speech is the progenitor of action
And all those solemn makings and unmakings,
Those untried treaties and alliances,
Are not less tangible or permanent
Than cornerstones or plaques on public buildings.
The truth is otherwise, but in the light
That streams across my sofa in the morning,
A sentence spoken forty years ago
Can echo with the resonance of rosewood
And seem as recent as the latest news.
'You're not *my* son.' It came without a warning.
And I, the newly disinherited,
Sitting across from her, could hardly know
Whether to take her angry words to heart
Or let them go, so level was her tone.
It was, I trust, no act commensurate
With that remark which set it into motion.
A startled hare, it bolted from the bushes
And then was off – a disappearing fluff
Of white. Not so its psychic indentation,
Which shows no sign of wear or weathering,
Its colours changing slightly with the years,

Its shape intact. On Lower Baggot Street
I heard my inner voice repeating it
As though it were the remnant of a mantra
And I, the unbeliever, were for once
Believing in the power of the word
To outlast depredations and erosions
And speak its meanings even to the grave.
Yet what could be less solid than the voice
That spoke these words – a voice that in its prime
Rang out with epithets and imprecations
But at the end grew thin and timorous –
A weary walker, trudging in and out
Of what is often called reality,
Remembering her savings to the dollar
But jumbling cousins, uncles, aunts, and friends
And spelling even the smallest words aloud.
Holding her hand and listening for hours,
Her fellow patients bleating in their corners,
The air a stifling blend of disinfectants,
I seldom spoke – but was once more her son,
Our worst fears forgotten or denied,
Our differences resolving in a bond
Beyond our speech or conscious understanding.

V

Thy will be done, intones the congregation,
As if it were as effortless as breathing
To let that lust for absolute control,
For order in the chambers of the heart

And purpose in the churnings of the world,
Dispel itself in painless exhalations
And by an act of sufferance allow
Its crusts to be dispersed across the water.
Not that it can't happen in the still
And speechless centre of an ordered mind –
Nor that a mind as willful as my own
Must be forever pinioned to volition.
Rather that these shiftings to and fro,
These turnings and returnings of the will
Across its own habitual terrain,
Will be suspended only for a time
Before the beast that calls itself the mind
Gets up to fetch its meal and buy its paper
And render its unqualified opinion.
The water will hold you up, I told myself
And for the better portion of an hour
I let myself subscribe to that belief.
Taking my evening constitutional
Down Gilford Road and out along the Strand,
I entertained the notion that those waves
Travelling the width of the Atlantic
And entering the depths of Dublin Bay
Were present at my moment of conception
And had for fifty years transported me
From one discrete occasion to another.
It was at most a fleeting fantasy,
Disrupted by the screeching of the tram
And the sight of dirty children flinging sand.
But for the brief duration of that dream
I heard a semblance of my father's voice

Speaking a soft endearment to my mother
And saw that in the matter of my birth,
As in the framing of my destiny,
There was no law nor order nor control
But only instinct, chance, and circumstance
Converging in an ever-changing pattern,
To which I still attach my signature
And lend the favour of an Irish blessing
But haven't the prerogative to alter
Or the temerity to call my own.

Notes

For the historical material in these poems I am indebted to Anthony Cronin's *Dead as Doornails* (Dolmen, 1976), Terence Brown's *Ireland: A Social and Cultural History, 1922-1985* (Fontana, 1985), Pauline Bracken's *Light of Other Days: A Dublin Childhood* (Mercier, 1992), Martin Morrissey's *Land of My Cradle Days* (O'Brien, 1990), Tom MacDonagh's *My Green Age* (Poolbeg, 1986), *The Field Day Anthology of Irish Writing, vol. III* (Field Day Publications, 1991), and some seventy issues of *The Bell* (1940-54), edited by Seán O'Faoláin and Peadar O'Donnell.